what is anything if not everything

Amanda Zhang

BookLeaf Publishing

what is anything if not everything © 2022
Amanda Zhang

Presentation by *BookLeaf Publishing*

Web: www.bookleafpub.com

E-mail: info@bookleafpub.com

ISBN: 9789357449427

First edition 2022

to the one born in 62

& the one born in 00

where I am from

Adapted by Laura Harjo and Inspired by
"Where I'm From" by George Ella Lyon

I am from the background hums of the
refrigerator
from the ticks and tocks of the noisy living room
clock
and the place where it snows on the hill.

I am from the light wood laminate creaky floors
to the dark real wood that no longer makes a
peep.

I am from the flowers my mom nurtures every
morning,
the big maple where the road starts and ends.

I am from strong women,
and resilience,
from the one born in 62
and the one born in 95
a last name I wish to be rid of, but doing so
would make me different from the ones I
survived with.

I am from the kind of laughter that makes your
tummy hurt and sometimes even cry.

from "it will get better"
and *"m ho gang, mommy hye dye tang"*

I am from the wind that courses through my
veins,
the soil that grounds my feet,
the sun that kisses my cheeks
my lips
my neck.

I am from the park across the street,
the folds of homemade dumplings,
and the winter melon fish cake sticky rice ball
stew my mom makes, because she knows it's my
favourite.

from the growth through learning how great, and
how cruel, people can be,
the courage of choosing independence,
and the fact that timing may never be right – but
never be wrong, either.

I am from the old and new developed film
pictures tucked away in my mom's closets and
mine.

what's in a name

what's in a name?
a connection
a relation
a close meaning.

what's in a name?
language, culture,
family ties
ancestral roots –
or perhaps, lack of?

what's in a name?
Westernization
and
there's always an and
fitting the self into English letters
at least there are 26 letters to toss around
fitting the self into something "easy to
pronounce"
*but if the white man can't say it, you're doing it
wrong*
fitting the self into Western colonial society
Western
colonial
ways

what’s in a name?
who you are and who you want to be,
or
who you aren’t, who you want to forget

what’s in a name?

what’s in yours?

purest forms

I don't want anything in its purest form

I want silence mixed with a bang
I want yin mixed with yang

I want clean floors mixed with muddy paws
I want freewill mixed with self-laws

I want mascara mixed with tears
I want spontaneity mixed with fears

I want white bathtubs mixed with sandy feet
I want the solo mixed with the whole fleet

I want my head clear
but that's my biggest fear

I don't want anything in its purest form

the browns, yellows, purples, and blues,

squeeze me out of the tube
put pressure where you want

as long as the palette
is filled with each colour

we can make art

at first, the brush tickled
but now the wood just snaps

as long as you need me
I can always be stained

you can make art

you taught me these colours
I started to practice

colours I never liked
the browns, yellows, purples,
and blues.

I never really liked art.

desire & fire

Inspired by Zen (Renunciation/Letting Go) by Mark Zocchi, Buddha's Little Book of Life

a house, not a home.
mister sun, please course through me.
the soil is cold.

4:47pm

the wooden stairs
the ones I could see through each step of
the cold as stone floors
the ones I stand on with my little bare feet
the light that rushes in from the window by the front door
the kind that dances around only in the late afternoon

the late afternoon
when people are laughing upstairs
when people are playing outside
when people are working hard

working hard
to set an example
to prove a point
to be there

be there
be there to turn the key to the right, and unlock the front door
be there to let the light rush in, as they perform ballet all around

be there to hold my hand and help me climb.

until tomorrow,
at 4:47
pm.

the queen bed

the queen bed
was so big that 10 of me could have fit
though I would have never wanted 10 of
me to have to commit to the same bit

the blinds roll by the traction of pull
it's old, got holes, but the specks of bright light
reminds me of stars, convince me it's dark

I toss, I turn, but at the end what works
the best, is on my back when I can hold,
contain, the flood that knows too well its path

I hum, I drum, but as soft as I can
the verses I sing, the lyrics that ring,
is the voice that always sung me to sleep

I didn't always sing myself to sleep.

eye sensitivities

my eyes sting from the flashes in time
my eyes burn from the heat of crimes
my eyes begin to sink
for better,
for worse,
like the feeling,
like the story,
I desperately wish would end.

the screen door

the creeks of an old screen door
the springs that wear out in the cold
the glass that is frosted over
and the weight of myself in front of it.

the cracks of my skin, I could only now see
the rings in my head, I could only now hear
the mass of blood coursing, I could only
now feel
and the weight of my fist so close—
yet not heavy enough to fall forwards.

the trembling of my fists
my hips
my lips

I let the rusty springs do their job.

poor pours

I know that giving =/= getting
and that was never my intent
but it gets a little hard
when my hands are constantly empty

backward thoughts

peel back the layers
but just
be careful
you don’t want to
make yourself bleed

big 2

sometimes you don't need to be dealt all the
right cards
to play them right

a homage to home

I still remember, in second grade, when
my teacher taught me the difference be-
tween what is a house, and what is a home.

she told me houses were just made of bricks,
but home is where the heart is, where you're
safe.
so next time write home, where you're not
alone.
okay?

now this next part, I'm not sure, I never
was sure, if it really happened or not.
I asked, what if home doesn't feel that way?

did I ever look up at a face wide,
and speechless? was it hers, or really mine?
thoughts that fire, but I can never say.

I keep wondering if I have ever asked
maybe because I still want an answer.
a question so tender with surrender.

oh, how I bet she forgot this lesson
a little red underline, mistake, but
I still remember. I still remember.

comes & grows

it comes and goes like the waves
but also
like the cotton floating through the sky
like the wind whispering stories
like the sun that shines at all the right places
like the stars hiding up north
like the moon that always knows its time.

the front seat

the front seat
arms open
feet dangle
eyes that can't see past the dash
eyes that can see past the cart
smells of rough hands and buttered toast

the front seat
in 10 years
driving by
I see me
arms open, coming in late
as rough hands put me down
did you get a bite of toast?

the front seat
in 12 years
on the bus
I see me
seat belt on and laughing hard
matching smiles in still traffic
I wonder if his hands are soft.

fire & desire

the hole in the roof
opens up a clear crisp sky.
I think I am home.

resurgence

what is a world without sunlight and soil?
what is a world that is not starting to boil?
the things we're taught and never to question,
I scrub. but it still leaves an impression.

I'm sorry that we're running out of time.
the things we've done, the things we do: a crime.
we grab your hand at the edge of a cliff,
the one we pushed you down. what an epiph-
any.

the words you spoke, when all our ears were
plugged,
of love, respect, nation—never enough.
teachings of gratitude I'm thankful for,
reminds me time and time I don't need more.

what if the seven sins were replaced by
the seven grandfather teachings? mind's eye:
people over profit, only a wish.
planet over profit, one day. *miikwehc*.

the conditions of the human condition

what are the conditions
to the human condition?

can you explain them to me,
so I am ready?

what are the conditions
to the human condition?

can you let me know in advance,
so they don't laugh at me?

what are the conditions
to the human condition?

can you teach them to me,
so I can let the others know?

what are the conditions
to the human condition?

can you repeat them to me,
when I feel them
too strongly
too lightly
or feel like I do not want to feel at all?

what are the conditions
to the human condition?

where should I sign?

double exposure

my fingertips tread the surface of the shutter
waiting to click, only on what matters

I see her in the viewfinder
but I could never find her

she comes out
and lurks about

in the blurs
like words slurred

in each
double exposure

kin pt.1

you were always warm
even after all the storms
I bask in your light

kin pt.2

I follow your streams
I would, to all the extremes
you taught me to flow

www.ingramcontent.com/pod-product-compliance
Lightning Source LLC
Chambersburg PA
CBHW051759130826
49812CB00033B/1209
* 9 7 8 9 3 5 7 4 4 9 4 2 7 *